anythink

D0116693

States

UTAH

by Bridget Parker

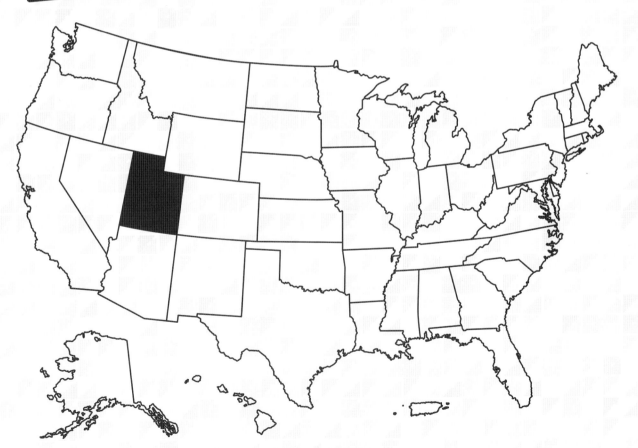

CAPSTONE PRESS
a capstone imprint

Next Page Books are published by Capstone Press,
1710 Roe Crest Drive, North Mankato, Minnesota 56003
www.mycapstone.com

Library of Congress Cataloging-in-Publication Data
Cataloging-in-publication information is on file with the Library of
Congress.
ISBN 978-1-5157-0432-4 (library binding)
ISBN 978-1-5157-0491-1 (paperback)
ISBN 978-1-5157-0543-7 (ebook PDF)

Editorial Credits
Jaclyn Jaycox, editor; Kazuko Collins and Katy LaVigne, designers;
Morgan Walters, media researcher; Tori Abraham, production specialist

Photo Credits
Alamy: Chronicle, 27; AP Images: Charles Tasnadi, middle 19;
Capstone Press: Angi Gahler, map 4, 7; CriaImages.com: Jay Robert
Nash Collection, top 18; Getty Images: Education Images, 17; Library
of Congress: Prints and Photographs Division, bottom 18, Harris
& Ewing, bottom 19; Newscom: Cal Sport Media/Chris Szagola, top
19; North Wind Picture Archives, 25; One Mile Up, Inc., flag, seal
23; Shutterstock: Aron Hsiao, 29, Blulz60, top right 21, Brocreative,
bottom right 8, Canadapanda, 13, Daniel Prudek, bottom left 21, Diane
Garcia, middle left 21, Doug Meek, 28, Everett Historical, 12, 26,
Gary Whitton, top 24, isak55, top left 21, Joe Seer, middle 18, Johnny
Adolphson, bottom left 8, 10, 14, Josemaria Toscano, 9, Joseph Sohm,
16, kojihirano, cover, Lee Prince, 15, LFRabanedo, top left 20, Maria
Jeffs, bottom 24, Mehmet Dilsiz, 11, Mitch Johanson, 5, 7, Pekka
Nikonen, bottom right 21, Randy Judkins, 6, Shulevskyy Volodymyr,
middle right 21, South Bay Lee, bottom left 20, Tom Reichner, right 20;
Wikimedia: Cory Maylett, top right 20

All design elements by Shutterstock

Printed and bound in China.
0316/CA21600187
012016   009436F16

TABLE OF CONTENTS

Want to take your research further? Ask your librarian if your school subscribes to PebbleGo Next. If so, when you see this helpful symbol (▸) throughout the book, log onto www.pebblegonext.com for bonus downloads and information.

LOCATION

Utah's position between Nevada and Colorado puts it in the heart of the West. As the 13th largest state, Utah stretches from Idaho and Wyoming in the north to Arizona and New Mexico in the south. The corners of New Mexico, Utah, Colorado, and Arizona all come together at a single point. This point is the only place in the country where four states meet. The Four Corners Monument marks this spot. Salt Lake City is Utah's capital and largest city. It is in the north-central part of the state. West Valley City and Provo are the next largest cities.

PebbleGo Next Bonus!
To print and label your own map, go to www.pebblegonext.com and search keywords:

UT MAP

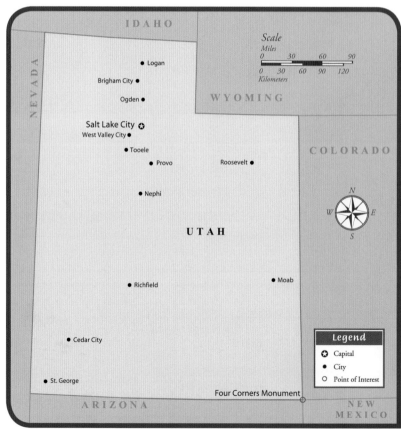

Until 1868 Salt Lake City was named Great Salt Lake City.

GEOGRAPHY

Utah has mountains, deserts, prairies, and canyons. Two ranges of the Rocky Mountains run through northeastern Utah. The Wasatch range comes down from the Idaho border. The Uinta Mountains stretch from Colorado westward toward Salt Lake City. Kings Peak, at 13,534 feet (4,125 meters) above sea level, is the highest point in Utah.

Western Utah is mostly desert, including the Great Salt Lake Desert. Southern Utah contains deep canyons, valleys, and interesting rock formations.

The Colorado River and the Green River are Utah's largest rivers. The state's biggest lake is filled with salt water instead of freshwater. The Great Salt Lake is one of the country's largest lakes.

PebbleGo Next Bonus! To watch a video about canyons and rock formations, go to www.pebblegonext.com and search keywords: UT VIDEO

The Great Salt Lake remains salty because it does not have an outlet.

Utah's Kings Peak is found in the Ashley National Forest.

Scale
Miles
0   30   60   90
0 30 60 90 120
Kilometers

N
W   E
S

Great Salt
Lake

Bear
Lake

GREAT SALT
LAKE DESERT

BASIN AND RANGE REGION

WASATCH RANGE

Flaming Gorge
Reservoir

Kings Peak

UINTA
MOUNTAINS

Utah
Lake

ROCKY MOUNTAINS

Green River

Sevier River

COLORADO PLATEAU

ARCHES
NATIONAL
PARK

Colorado River

CAPITOL REEF
NATIONAL
PARK

CANYONLANDS
NATIONAL
PARK

BRYCE CANYON
NATIONAL PARK

ZION NATIONAL
PARK

GRAND STAIRCASE-
ESCALANTE NATIONAL
MONUMENT

San Juan River

Lake Powell

Legend
▲ Highest Point
◯ Lake
🌲 Mountain Range
▇ National Park
▨ National
    Monument
〜 River

WEATHER

Temperatures in Utah are warm in the summer and cool in the winter. The average summer temperature is 69 degrees Fahrenheit (21 degrees Celsius). The average temperature in winter is 27°F (-3°C).

Average High and Low Temperatures (Salt Lake City, UT)

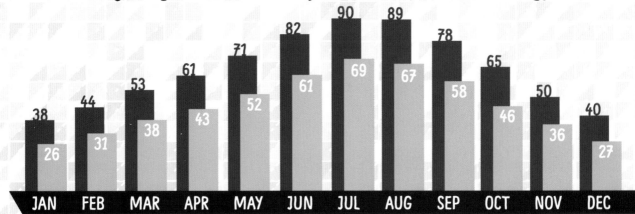

	JAN	FEB	MAR	APR	MAY	JUN	JUL	AUG	SEP	OCT	NOV	DEC
High	38	44	53	61	71	82	90	89	78	65	50	40
Low	26	31	38	43	52	61	69	67	58	46	36	27

LANDMARKS

Arches National Park

Tourists and hikers love to visit this park. It has more than 2,000 natural stone arches as well as many other interesting rock formations.

Great Salt Lake

Although few fish live in this salty lake, it is home to many birds. Sunbathing on white beaches, hiking the marshy islands, and sailing boats are popular recreation activities.

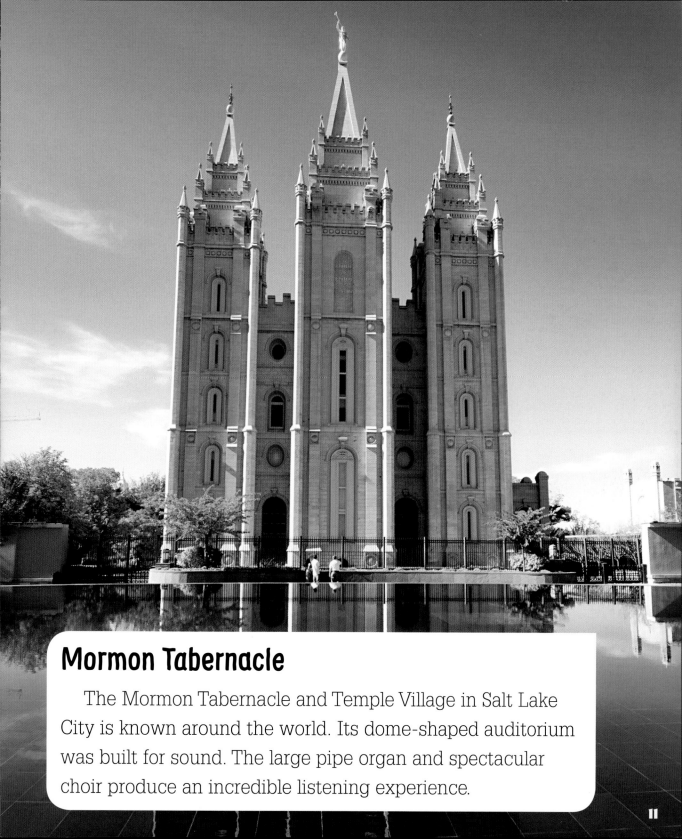

Mormon Tabernacle

The Mormon Tabernacle and Temple Village in Salt Lake City is known around the world. Its dome-shaped auditorium was built for sound. The large pipe organ and spectacular choir produce an incredible listening experience.

HISTORY AND GOVERNMENT

Brigham Young, shown with his family, founded Salt Lake City.

People have lived in Utah since ancient times. Ancient cultures existed in Utah long before the Pueblo culture arrived around the year 400. Many native groups lived in Utah over the next hundreds of years. Spanish explorers came through Utah in 1776. American and British trappers and fur traders made their way to Utah in the 1820s and 1830s. Utah's first permanent white settlers were Mormons seeking religious freedom. Mormon leader Brigham Young led settlers into the state in 1847. The U.S. government was slow to grant statehood to Utah. Many leaders disapproved of Mormon beliefs. In 1896 Utah finally became the 45th state.

Utah's state government has legislative, executive, and judicial branches. The legislative branch has two sections—the 29-member Senate and the 75-member House of Representatives. Utah's governor heads the executive branch. Judges and their courts make up the judicial branch.

Utah's state capitol building is located in Salt Lake City.

INDUSTRY

Manufacturing is a large industry in Utah. Companies make computer and office equipment, transportation equipment, medical equipment, and navigational systems. Many companies also make military products such as solid rocket fuel.

Despite all the rocks and canyons in Utah's landscape, the state still has a large agricultural industry. Farmers grow grasses and grains to feed livestock. They also grow potatoes, onions, other vegetables, and fruits. Beef cattle and milk are the leading products. Utah is also one of the top sheep-farming states.

Grown to feed cattle, hay is Utah's largest crop.

Mining is also an important part of Utah's economy. The state is rich in natural resources. Coal, natural gas, uranium, petroleum, and natural salts are all found in Utah. Valuable metals such as gold, silver, and copper are also mined.

The state of Utah ranks second in copper and magnesium compound mining.

POPULATION

Most Utahns have European ancestors. Many follow the Mormon religion of the first white settlers in Utah. Utah's jobs and recreation have brought other people to the state as well. The Hispanic population has been growing in recent years. There is a small population of African-Americans, Asians, and other races, but almost 80 percent of Utahns are white.

Though their numbers are small, many American Indian cultures live in Utah. The Navajo, Ute, Goshute, Southern Paiute, and Shoshone still have an important presence in the state.

Population by Ethnicity

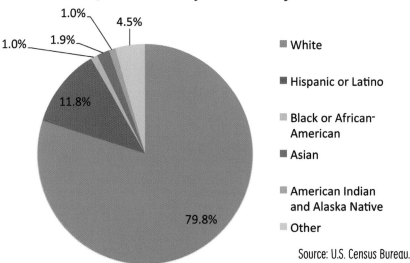

1.0%
4.5%
1.0%
1.9%
11.8%
79.8%

- White
- Hispanic or Latino
- Black or African-American
- Asian
- American Indian and Alaska Native
- Other

Source: U.S. Census Bureau.

FAMOUS PEOPLE

Butch Cassidy (1866–1908) was an outlaw in the Old West. He was born Robert Leroy Parker near Beaver. He is known for robbing banks and trains and leading the Wild Bunch Gang.

Chelsie Hightower (1989–) is a professional dancer. She has performed on the television programs *So You Think You Can Dance* and *Dancing with the Stars*. She was raised in Orem.

Brigham Young (1801–1877) led the first settlement in Utah. He led the Mormon settlers and was governor of Utah Territory from 1851 to 1858.

Steve Young (1961–) is a retired NFL quarterback. He won multiple MVP awards in his time as a player. He was born in Salt Lake City.

John Willard Marriott (1900–1985) was born near Ogden. As a businessman, he developed the world's largest chain of hotels and food services companies.

Philo Taylor Farnsworth (1906–1971) was an inventor who pioneered television. He was born near Beaver.

STATE SYMBOLS

Tree

blue spruce

Flower

sego lily

Bird

California seagull

Animal

Rocky Mountain elk

PebbleGo Next Bonus! To make a dessert with Utah's official state snack, go to www.pebblegonext.com and search keywords:

UT RECIPE

Vegetable

Spanish sweet onion

Folk Dance

square dance

Cooking Pot

longhorn

Fruit

cherry

Insect

honeybee

Gem

topaz

FAST FACTS

STATEHOOD
January 4, 1896

CAPITAL ☆
Salt Lake City

LARGEST CITY •
Salt Lake City

SIZE
82,170 square miles (212,819 square kilometers) land area (2010 U.S. Census Bureau)

POPULATION
2,900,872 (2013 U.S. Census estimate)

STATE NICKNAME
Beehive State

STATE MOTTO
"Industry"

STATE SEAL

The Utah legislature approved the state seal in 1896. On a shield in the middle is a beehive, which stands for hard work. Sego lilies, representing peace, surround the hive. Below the hive is the year 1847. This was the year Mormons first came to Utah. Above the beehive is the word "Industry," the state motto. Above the motto are six arrows and a bald eagle, representing protection. Two U.S flags surround the shield. Around the border are the words "The Great Seal of the State of Utah." The date 1896, at the bottom, is when Utah became a state.

PebbleGo Next Bonus!
To print and color
your own flag, go to
www.pebblegonext.com
and search keywords:
UT FLAG

STATE FLAG

Utah's original state flag was adopted in 1896. It was later revised and made official in 1913. The flag is dark blue with a yellow circle in the middle. Inside the circle is the state seal. A beehive and the word "Industry" are in a shield in the center to symbolize hard work. Lilies around the hive stand for peace. An eagle and arrows represent protection. Two American flags decorate the edges of the shield. Two dates are on the flag. 1847 is the year the Mormon people came to Utah. 1896 is the year Utah became a state.

MINING PRODUCTS

copper, natural gas, petroleum, coal, gold, magnesium, molybdenum, potash, salt, sand and gravel, silver

MANUFACTURED GOODS

metal, chemicals, computer and electronic products, petroleum and coal products, food and beverage products

FARM PRODUCTS

milk, beef, turkeys, eggs, hogs, sheep, cattle feed, wheat, barley, corn, apples, peaches, potatoes

PROFESSIONAL SPORTS TEAMS

Real Salt Lake (MLS)
Utah Jazz (NBA)

PebbleGo Next Bonus!
To learn the lyrics to
the state song, go to
www.pebblegonext.com
and search keywords:
UT SONG

UTAH TIMELINE

400 — Pueblo people settle in Utah.

1620 — The Pilgrims establish a colony in the New World in present-day Massachusetts.

1776 — Spanish explorers travel through Utah.

1847 — Mormons reach the Great Salt Lake Valley.

1857–1858

Mormons and the U.S. government fight each other in the Utah War.

1861–1865

The Union and the Confederacy fight the Civil War.

1896

Utah is granted statehood.

1916

Workers complete the Utah State Capitol in Salt Lake City.

1914–1918

World War I is fought; the United States enters the war in 1917.

1939–1945

World War II is fought; the United States enters the war in 1941.

1952 Workers find uranium deposits near Moab.

1983 A group of Utahns start the Novell software company with an idea for a new computer program.

1996 President Bill Clinton establishes the Grand Staircase-Escalante National Monument. It covers a large area of southern Utah.

2002
Salt Lake City hosts the 2002 Olympic Winter Games.

2013
On April 10 a large rockslide pushes 165 million tons (150 million metric tons) of debris into Bingham Canyon Mine and triggers small earthquakes in the mining pit.

2015
In September, the deadliest flood in state history claims 20 lives in southern Utah.

Glossary

agriculture *(AG-ruh-kul-chur)*—the science of growing crops

canyon *(KAN-yuhn)*—a deep, narrow valley

executive *(ig-ZE-kyuh-tiv)*—the branch of government that makes sure laws are followed

industry *(IN-duh-stree)*—a business which produces a product or provides a service

judicial *(joo-DISH-uhl)*—to do with the branch of government that explains and interprets the laws

legislature *(LEJ-iss-lay-chur)*—a group of elected officials who have the power to make or change laws for a country or state

natural resource *(NACH-ur-uhl REE-sorss)*—a material found in nature that is useful to people

navigation *(NAV-uh-gay-shun)*—using instruments and charts to find your way in a ship or other vehicle

petroleum *(puh-TROH-lee-uhm)*—an oily liquid found below the earth's surface used to make gasoline, heating oil, and many other products

prairie *(PRAIR-ee)*—a large area of flat or rolling grassland with few or no trees

recreation *(rek-ree-AY-shuhn)*—the games, sports, hobbies, etc. that people enjoy in their spare time

Read More

Felix, Rebecca. *What's Great About Utah?* Our Great States. Minneapolis: Lerner Publications, 2015.

Ganeri, Anita. *United States of America: A Benjamin Blog and His Inquisitive Dog Guide.* Country Guides. Chicago: Heinemann Raintree, 2015.

Sanders, Doug. *Utah.* It's My State! New York: Cavendish Square Publishing, 2016.

Internet Sites

FactHound offers a safe, fun way to find Internet sites related to this book. All of the sites on FactHound have been researched by our staff.

Here's all you do:

Visit *www.facthound.com*

Type in this code: 9781515704324

Super-cool stuff! Check out projects, games and lots more at **www.capstonekids.com**

Critical Thinking Using the Common Core

1. Utah has many different landscapes including mountains, deserts, prairies, and canyons. Which two mountain ranges run through the state? Hint: Use the map on page 7 to help. (Craft and Structure)

2. Mining is an important part of Utah's economy. The state is rich in natural resources. What are three natural resources found in Utah? (Key Ideas and Details)

3. Arches National Park is a landmark in Utah. What do you think attracts visitors here? (Integration of Knowledge and Ideas)

Index